About the Author

Anthony Superina was born in Australia a millennium ago. Many who have encountered Anthony would refer to him as mysterious and quiet. For those very few close to him would disagree with him being quiet. When he isn't enjoying times with those closest to him, you will almost always find him exploring his curiosities.

Within the Margin of Error

Anthony Superina

Within the Margin of Error

Vanguard Press

VANGUARD PAPERBACK

© Copyright 2024
Anthony Superina

The right of Anthony Superina to be identified as author of this work has been asserted by him in accordance with the Copyright, Designs and Patents Act 1988.

All Rights Reserved

No reproduction, copy or transmission of this publication may be made without written permission.
No paragraph of this publication may be reproduced, copied or transmitted save with the written permission of the publisher, or in accordance with the provisions of the Copyright Act 1956 (as amended).

Any person who commits any unauthorised act in relation to this publication may be liable to criminal prosecution and civil claims for damages.

A CIP catalogue record for this title is available from the British Library.

ISBN 978 1 80016 938 8

Vanguard Press is an imprint of
Pegasus Elliot Mackenzie Publishers Ltd.
www.pegasuspublishers.com

First Published in 2024

Vanguard Press
Sheraton House Castle Park
Cambridge England

Printed & Bound in Great Britain

Serendipitously we met… You saw through me, the man who was trying to hide. You are an important part of my life and without you a part of my life, this never eventuates. You are the inspiration behind the emotions and the words.

Contents

DESPONDENCY FORTIFIED	13
2020	15
BUT TO DREAM	16
WIDOWED	17
ABYSS	18
MY LIFE	19
INTO THE SHADOWS	20
WITHIN	21
THE INVISIBLE	23
REM	24
LONG	LOST	LOVE	25
SWEEPING	27
HOLLOW BLUES	28
THAT'S REALITY	30
TIME… TICKING	32
SUDDENLY	33
HELLO, MY OLD FRIEND	34
CONFLICTION LOST	35
CRIPPLED INSIDE	36
TRUTHS	37
ENIGMA	38
LEGACY	39
SERENDIPITOUS INTERVENTION	40
ONE MOMENT	41
MS. L	42
DELICIOSA	43
FAREWELL 2020	44

2021	45
BELLEZZA SENSUALE	46
VISION	47
HAVE A LITTLE FAITH	48
WHEREVER YOU ARE, YOU ARE HERE	49
BONITA	50
MAGICAL… MYSTERIOUS	52
THE APPLE OF MY EYE	54
ONE	56
ANJO	57
BEYOND THE BLUE	58
ETERNALLY	59
FOR I WILL	60
INNER LIGHT	61
CALM ME	62
DIA DOS NAMORADOS	63
ENERGY	64
EXQUISITE	65
FREE	66
FROM ME TO YOU	67
LONGING	68
MEU AMOR	69
MEU PROMESSA	70
PALPABLE	71
PASSION. INTIMACY. LOVE	72
TOUCH	73
SERENDIPITOUS	74
PROMISES	75
THREE MINUTES	76

HEART'S DESIRE	77
ONE	78
I WANT YOU	79
LONELY HEART	80

DESPONDENCY FORTIFIED

My heart, morphing into stone, depleted of its warmth.

Once nourished with passion… excited with love
Intoxicated through seduction, pleasured through intimacy.

No longer.

For hope is dying
Despair… dawning
No vibrancy any more.

To fall asleep
My head upon my pillow
Drifting… floating upon a stream of time.
One frequency engaging my mind
I wonder how it feels
The soul, slipping away
Disconnecting from the physical.

Shall I feel coldness?
Will numbness be that of my final emotion?

An eternity of purgatory
May my conclusion, generate that of harmony.
May it bring forth the birth of a soul,
A soul in which this world would benefit.

Intuition dictates my days are numbered
A lifetime ago, serendipity intervened
For home is where the heart is,
And my heart is calling me home.

2020

Loneliness frazzles
The mind, the body and the soul.

Sounds muted
Outside of the sound of silence…
    Deafening!

To but lay my touch
Upon warm, silky and soft skin…
    Fanciful.

Tragedy filled, 2019 exits
Scarred, isolated, lonely, scared…
    2020 begins.

I know not of this year born
Heartache and sorrow lingers.

Here I am… merely waiting.

BUT TO DREAM

What hope that resided, has since waned
What faith possessed, now diminished
To feel the sensual touch… a woman's caress
The embrace of love, but a foolish dream.

To feel love once more within this unfilled heart
But a fanciful delusion.

WIDOWED

Loneliness: for the heart desires love.
Isolation: for the mind seeks stimulation.
    Eroticism: for the soul craves passion and intimacy.

Lost: for I know not who I am without you.
Fear: for knowing I may never feel love once more.
    Desolate: for opportunity doesn't always arrive.

Acceptance: for I am introverted and undesired.
Reality: for my time is up.
    Dreaming: for the day we're reunited.

ABYSS

My existence, the cause of someone's pain, a fate I bear each day
Often misunderstood, underappreciated, undesired
The green-eyed beast; spawned from siblings and friends.

A childhood denied… lost.

Life is that of purpose
I have searched far and wide… unfulfilled.

I have lived, caring and supporting of others, I know not how to live.

I have loved. I have lost.

I guess I wasn't meant for these times.

MY LIFE

A curse.
For these eyes see the subtle changes
For sweet words whispered, reveal the revelation hidden.

The battle.
Turbulence within; to declare or to ponder in silence; distant!
For this heart of mine once devastated, scarcely withstanding
It cannot brave any further pain.
Few hearts are synchronised, beating as one.

The sacrifice.
I would be that of a coward to inflict pain;
For I know the consequence and thus, the reverberation
For it's most fitting, what heart of thine remains
Ingests all pains, 'til it slows and beats no more.

My life.
I have lived for love
To be desired as I covet the one whom I gave my heart and soul.

Take it.
For in this world, love is not enough.

INTO THE SHADOWS

But a mere individual amongst billions
   Invisible.

Crucified by siblings, forgotten by friends
   Faded.

Alone, surrounded by a crowd, imperceptible to the world
   Isolated.

I have loved, only to watch her die
   Alone.

Who am I?
But a mere individual; a wasted existence.

Quiet and by surprise I entered; unnoticed and silently I'll
   leave…
Into the shadows.

WITHIN

The sun no longer rises
Once azure skies, dark and ominous.

Shades of grey consume the vibrancy
Aromas, absent from nature.

Gone is the giddy smile, reminiscent of a little child.

No conversations, no cheering or jeering, no laughter, the
    sound of silence echoes.

The stark contrast of home
No vision; blinded by the emptiness.

The intensity of the deluge
In the distance, the thundery orgasm grows.

Cold, the naked bed
Absent of caressing warmth… chilling.

The cravings, the desires, the needs… tantalising.
The loneliness, the haunting; all consuming.

As I sit here, merely ageing
Unrecognisable, the man in the mirror.

My written word, my eternal voice.

For my solemn eyes look upon the world, and I wonder…

THE INVISIBLE

For is invisibility confined to the realm of science-fiction?
   Yet here I am…

Invisible.

REM

Days drag in passing, nights linger in dawning
Time seemingly frozen
The mind absorbing the world encompassing.

I've witnessed the origins of cynicism
Egotism, narcissism and audacious self-promotion Openly
    flaunted, absent of repercussion.

What hope that remains for humanity… dwindling
For the darkness settles before the dawn.

LONG | LOST | LOVE

Never could I have conceived, to love with all my essence
For it's my love and my life to give.

Within you, I live
Without you, I'm crippled inside
The dream, the dream is over.

Here I am, losing control, shivering within
Here I am, alone, struggling without you by my side.

How do I pick up the pieces?
How do I find love again, when I know not of this peculiar world?

For I know I'm an aberration
For I am not, a man desired.

No one cares for your name
No one understands the soul
No one cares to know the man, behind the blue eyes.

Within the shattered pieces of the mirror, hundreds of razors
Shimmering beneath the morning light.

"For those with the warmest hearts, feel all pain."

SWEEPING

The distance slowly grows
The thrill of the chase… over.

Time, ever so fleeting, continuously sweeping.

This heart of mine, no longer whole
What pieces remain, dying.

Undesired. Unloved. Unwanted.

HOLLOW BLUES

A year removed, a year…

Words no longer flow.

No longer am I the man I once knew
No longer do I recognise the reflection haunting the mirror.

Who am I?
Who am I without you?
Who am I supposed to be?
Who am I supposed to be without you?

The absence of love, the heart, hollow.

The absence of intimacy, passion wanes.

Every morning the same… loneliness
Memories replayed; biding time.

Every night, the same… coldness
An empty bed, no comfort, no warmth.

Thoughts of her occupy my mind
The realisation I may never be loved
The realisation, I'm old and undesired
The realisation of a life; empty and lonely.

    I just want to die.

THAT'S REALITY

Why am I here?
I have nothing left to give.
Here I sit, waiting for the day.

Why did I meet her? Why did I fall in love?
Why was she so cruelly snuffed, from this very existence?

Here, I'm left; with what purpose? For I am without purpose.
For I'm without hope.

The loneliness; dark and cold.
It haunts my soul; no escape.
I'm reminded of the love, the laughter, the passion, the sex, and the tears.

No longer do I recognise the man -- old, greying, rugged… reclusive
Happiness, but a term within a dictionary.
The realisation… the realisation…
Destined to a life secluded, surrounded by loneliness and pain.

I know not of the time remaining, although I feel it waning
The loneliness, the desire, the anguish -- I cannot withstand much more.

What's the use in waking, without you.

TIME... TICKING

Why am I seen as undesirable?
Is it that of my inner self or the physical?

Why am I unable to find love?
Never first... always last;
What little interest, spurred through pity.

Why do I feel so lost?
Could it be this loneliness that lingers; consuming?

Forty-three years, adrift...
For I know not of the man within,
Always down-trodden, under foot of the green-eyed monster.
And this – where the story ends.

SUDDENLY

The frailty of life skulks amongst the shadows
    Lying in wait patiently… opportunistic.

A second hand sweeps across an old schoolhouse face
    Timed precision… eroding.

Dawns muted early light… penetrating
    Life begins awakening from its slumber.

Clouds, sporadic across cerulean skies
    The birds sing, greeting the brand-new day.

Saltwater wells as a baby cries
    Tears of anguish echo of love's sudden loss
Sullen hearts… overwhelmed.

Reminders endure. Memories live.

HELLO, MY OLD FRIEND

Vanity flourishing, hatred all-consuming
Decency but a forgotten word
Humanity cannibalising itself.

Ugliness disguised within filters, intentions decisive and impish
Characters revealed within sub-text
A world, self-absorbed.

Connections… wireless
    Emotions… moot
Interactions… digital
    Sexuality… confusion.

The sun no longer rises; darkness blanketing
Blue mist surrounds the soul
No bell, book or candle can rectify this.

For this world is not mine, never it was
My continuance… doubtful
In the absence of intimacy and love.

CONFLICTION LOST

This world continues to spiral
Everywhere, double standards and ineptitude, litter political corridors and halls.

No longer can I see the light that once shimmered
The future bright now enveloped within a heavy fog.

At the crossroads I stand, motionless, feet overhanging the precipice
For this heart and soul of mine, torn.

Greatness stands before her
Thousands look to her for guidance and care
Who am I to distract!

I know not where I stand
I've given all that I have, now exhausted

To love… to be loved.
To touch… to be touched.

Have I merely fooled myself?

CRIPPLED INSIDE

How can I clear my mind
Her words linger, meandering…
Words lashed in anger maybe forgiven, although never forgotten.

Within, my emotions rage; at war
To love her. To believe in her.

Intimate advances dismissed, middle ground out-stretching
Attention diminished, affection fading
The thrill of the chase subsiding.

Trust absent, the pain and emptiness…
What heart and soul that survived, unconditionally, I give.

Our paths intersected…

I have lived, loved and lost.
This heart can endure no more.

For in the end…

TRUTHS

To hear words hidden
Chilling… bone shattering;
Realisations of decisions past, realisation of coming tomorrows.

No one to blame, but me. No one to shame, but me.
For the fool I am. What is, will be.
Security I cannot deliver
Haunted by decisions past
Demons circle, the hell mouth awaits.

History defined. Loneliness destined.

I know not of the reflection these eyes staring upon my soul;
Through the mirrored pieces, one's shattered fate.

'Tis the moment…

For love extinguishes…

ENIGMA

For the words scribed, shall fade with time
For this weary face hidden in sight, shall erode with time
For the unfamiliar sound of this voice, shall fall silent with time
For this name, shall be forgotten with time.

For the night is darkest before first light

    For I, an enigma.

LEGACY

The rising sun, a new day begun
With the setting sun, a day set to rest
Each cycle, I continue to age
As time is no friend of mine.

To discover love again… a feeble fable
To leave a legacy… forever passed
What legacy that may exist
Shall cease upon my last exhale.

In the end, life continues with and without us
Photos lost
Memories fade
Names forgotten.

SERENDIPITOUS INTERVENTION

Her flowing hair, accented with waves, draping across her exposed shoulders.
Her eyes; a tale of two stories
Her radiating smile
Soothing, warming, welcoming.

Subtle and soft; her lips inviting
To but taste her sweet lips: desirable.
The sound of her voice: mesmerising
Her words… passionate and honest.

Her dedication: inspiring.
Her wounded heart, stronger than she realises.

A classic… a masterpiece
Not even the great Michelangelo
Could not have sculpted such perfection.
Her beauty… her curves: enticing and inviting.
I patiently await the day
To embrace the physical… to feel her heart beat.

She stoked the ember deep within
The flame I thought extinguished, again burns, fuelled with passion.

ONE MOMENT

Beyond the façade, her eyes engaged -- the man… the soul behind the blue eyes
She read the words penned from the deepest depths
Between and beyond the text, my desire.

Her words penned raw and honest; oozing warmth
Something endearing and yet familiar
Caressing that of my fragile soul.

Thoughts endlessly meander, nerves stimulated… uncontrollable
Her voice… soothing, her eyes… mesmerising.

Her presence brought laughter
Awakening the passion, shackled and suppressed
Her smile, seducing
Stirring me in a way I once felt before.

I know not of the future
Yet, I know serendipity skulks
Whether the premise of friendship or greater, our paths diverged; intersecting for a reason.

MS L

There she was, appearing serendipitously, out of the deep
    Pacific blue
A light... a light illuminating the darkness.

Amongst the sadness and frustration, her kindness... her
    passion
Insatiably magnetic!

To hear her sultry voice... to gaze into her sexy eyes
A familiar feeling stirs within
Passion... hunger... desire
Longing... wanting... needing

To see her, my knees weaken
    To hold her tight
To run my hands through her hair
    To hold her hand in mine

To read her words before I close my eyes
To awaken to visions of her.
She has captivated my heart
For the passion and desire burns deeply.

DELICIOSA

Although the greatest of oceans keeps us apart
You are always near me... with me... a part of me
Two distant lands... two souls... one love, the sound of
　　your voice is music to my ears
To just see you smile illuminates the darkest of days

Your words... your gifts, fuel the flames burning within
　　How I yearn to gaze into your sultry eyes
To gaze upon that gorgeous smile

Igniting the passion, you make me feel alive
You are of inspiration

I give you my soul and my heart
Envisioning you
I want you
I love you

FAREWELL 2020

A year chaotic
    A year of uncertainty and isolation
A year historically referenced 1820… 1920… 2020…

Upheaval… instigated
    Humanity… crumbling
Greed… embellished

2020, a year eternally etched
Humanities Achilles… nature's vigour

2021

A year foreseen
    A year of fledgling love
    A year optimistic
Susceptible hearts shall declare

Magic… ingrained
Desires… insistent
Intimacy… brewing

2021, a year committed to love
A year ardent… a season for lovers

BELLEZZA SENSUALE

There's something about her eyes
Soft and alluring; windows to her soul.

Her long natural locks, reminiscent of flowing falls.

The magic of golden hour, her figure silhouetted
Her curves… seducing.

Her beauty emanating passion
Her soul, beautiful.

Within her heart, there's something that seduces my soul
    Her voice… captivates
Conjuring intimate thoughts and future dreams.

Her smile radiates, her lips subtle
Her presence… intoxicating!

VISION

Her smile from the brush of da Vinci
From the palette of Renoir, her eyes
From the hands of Michelangelo, her figure.

Her skin, soft as the finest Angora silk
Caressing sheets of Mulberry silk.

The vision of her... exciting... inviting... enticing.
    Sensual and seductive.
Her hips, curvaceous
These eyes cannot avert from such exquisite beauty.

Upon this hot summer night, she lay restless, window ajar,
    a gentle evening breeze blows
Drifting ever so daintily.

The emotion within thine heart and soul... invigorating!
    For her image upon thine eyes... divine!

HAVE A LITTLE FAITH

For these eyes to see the saltwater well in yours, my heart breaks
For I wish to wipe those tears away;
To hold you tight.

For these eyes to gaze into yours, to see the pain and frustration, my body wanes
For I spurn, to see you this way
If only I could absorb your pain
For you need not feel this anguish.

For the sadness will end; the sun will shine
For a faded orchid will bloom once more
Even the dimmest of places
A glimmer of light… penetrates.

For you may now feel weak, yet these eyes see;
You are replete of spirit, courage and determination.
    Remember, you need not walk this journey alone.
    Forte. Inteligente. Determinado. Bonita.

WHEREVER YOU ARE, YOU ARE HERE

For I dream living was easy with eyes closed, for each
    night I lay down, and close my eyes
Thoughts relentlessly meandering my weary mind.

Her pain coursing through my soul
Not a cell within this shell doesn't feel.
Her withdrawing… haunting.
Fourteen thousand kilometres
This modern world, imprisoned by humanities greed.

But to smell her essence as she nears
    To feel her heart beat in embrace
To but taste her sweetness upon her subtle lips.

To dream of a life without you…
    That, I dare not dream.

BONITA

To awaken to the morning sun
To feel your breath upon my face
Feeling the beat of our hearts.

In the evening, beneath southern skies
To see the love in your eyes.

DO YOU BELIEVE IN MAGIC?

The gentle pitter-patter of rain falling, distant rumbles of
    thunder rolling
The darkened room illuminated
Lightning branching across evening skies; to lay with you,
    resting in my arms
Drifting into a world of slumber… perfect!

Dream, sweet dreams for you and me.

With the rise of the morning star, the break of a new day
    dawning, the birds sing.

To awaken, holding you
    To see you smile
To wipe the golden slumbers from your eyes
To feel your body stretch
The tension… the release.

MAGICAL... MYSTERIOUS

2020, a year chaotic; a year of unknowns
The world we knew, forever altered, history repeated
Freedom pillaged by hands tainted with gluttony.

Out of the blue, a delicate glimmer, her essence illuminating
Her spirit, free! Her smile, magnetic! Her inner beauty, exquisite!
Never could I have dreamt my feelings could flourish. Two souls akin
She touched me without physical touch, my withering flame, feverous once more!

This heart of mine, robust in beat.

Patiently she waited, her heart enraptured
For these eyes, could not see.

2021, a year of promise, a time of hope
For the emotion strengthens.

Two distant lands;

The green, the gold and the blue
The sparkling waters and the shimmering sands.

That moment longed for
To kiss her, to hold her
She knows not what she does to me.

A lover of nature
The heart of a mermaid
With the soul of a lioness.

The sun sets in her eyes
The ocean runs through her veins
For today, I love her more than yesterday!

THE APPLE OF MY EYE

Time could not move more slowly, for the hands upon the face have frozen.

Two spirited souls, meandering;
A single serendipitous moment, all that was needed.

Her beautiful smile… adored
Her touching words and sexy tones… irresistible
Her glimmering eyes… seducing.

For I was blind, but now I can see.

Fear not of the past, nor the future;
Take my hand, for the future is ours, come see.

No matter the distance
You are here, as I am there
For you touched me, as I touched you.

Within two souls; passion grows
Desires yearn.

For you are the apple of my eye
For you are the mermaid and I, the sea
For you are my weakness, as you are my strength.

Close your eyes -- envision the moment to be
The sound of the ocean lapping the shore -- to feel the sand
    beneath your feet
Whilst standing beneath the pale moon light.

To gaze into one another's eyes --

ONE

For you are my favourite person.

Two continents… one hemisphere
Two colours; green and gold… one almighty ocean
7.9 billion people
200 billion galaxies
An infinite universe.

And you are the only one!

ANJO

The night is darkest before the dawn
The morning is brightest as the sun emerges.

The morning star; her aura emanating
Alluring, her soft brown eyes; gorgeous, her sweet smile.

Through these blue eyes, angelic visions
Behind these blue eyes, the love… the future.

BEYOND THE BLUE

Out the blue, you appeared
You inflamed my heart and touched my soul.
This heart of mine covets no one, but you!
This restless soul shall find its peace, the day our bodies entwine in embrace!

ETERNALLY

My love for you burns fiercely
Never will it slow, never shall it extinguish
For eternal is the flame.

FOR I WILL

I will fill your darkness with light
    I will replace your sadness with that of happiness.
I will raise you when you're feeling blue
    I will be your guiding light when you are lost.

Never will I hurt you.
Never will I abandon you.

For I will always love you.

INNER LIGHT

I want you on your saddest days
I want you on your happiest days
I want you on your bluest days

I want you…

I want you early in the morning
I want you by the ocean's roar

I want you…

I want to taste your sweet lips
I want to hold you in my arms

I want you…

I want to uncontrollably laugh with you
I want to wipe away your tears
I want to be the reason for your spontaneous smile

I want you.

CALM ME

Calm me with your tender embrace
Soothe me with your exquisite kisses
Centre me with your words of love
    Tame the wild passion within.

Tease me with your sensuous voice
    Seduce me with your provocative eyes
Arouse me with your gorgeous physique
Love me like you've loved no other.

Stimulate my mind with your wisdom
Draw me nearer with your dreams and nightmares.

DIA DOS NAMORADOS

As long as the sun continues to burn
And the moon shimmers upon the ocean waves, I will love
 you.

As long as the flooding rains saturate;
Quenching the earth after years of drought, I will love you
 until the end of days.

When the moon no longer shines
And the sun exhausted, burns no more
My love for you will remain forevermore.

ENERGY

I long for your lips, that sweet kiss
I want to feel a sense of intoxication
As you leave these lips wanting.

I crave your soft touch, to feel your skin caressing mine
Your drifting touch, tingling my every nerve.

I love you with every essence of who I am
I love you with all that I hope to be
Within you, a piece of my heart and soul, yearning for the
    day our energies entwine.

I may not be the first to have captivated your heart, yet, I
    hope to be your last.

EXQUISITE

Azure skies, abundantly endless
    Absent of cloud, devoid of definition.

A spider's web, geometric in design
    Dew-dropped kissed
Scintillating, by dawn's early light.

Shimmering oceans... proliferating views... undulating
    onto shore
Lapping sandstone, soothing tones.

Blinding white
Adrift, a solitary flake, endlessly tumbling.

Ambient Sol
Divergent skies; resplendent vibrance
Orgasmic grandeur disseminating.

Alluring and sensuous... sweet and luscious
Silky and firm
Warm and wet.

FREE

Fear not the future
Trust in your heart; trust in us
For you have touched my soul
To have seen beyond the blue
Gazing into the windows of my soul

FROM ME TO YOU

This unconditional heart, I give to you.

The penetrating light in your darkest moments
    The shimmering light, I am.

At your weakest, these arms will support you, to keep you
    safe and warm.

These hands will hold your hands, warming and
    reassuring.
These fingers will wipe the tears that shall fall
My lips pressed against the softness of yours
Feel the emotion
Enjoy the passion.

For your light is that of my love.

LONGING

Every night I crawl beneath the sheets

Alone.

Each morning I rise

Alone.

My love, far from my side
Her presence, deep within my heart

Lockdowns!
Closures!
Curfews!
Mandates!
Separation!

Lovers isolated
Lovers longing
Lovers separated

Fleeting is time
Precious is love

Together, we will be…

MEU AMOR

Calm my passion with your gentle embrace
Comfort me with your gorgeous smile
Soothe my mind with your sultry voice
Seduce my soul with your passionate kiss

Avow your hands to meander
    Avow your succulent lips to explore
Avow your chocolaty eyes to illustrate

Sense the intimacy, unleash the tension
    Celebrate the love

Uninhibited
 Unbound
  Unstoppable

MEU PROMESSA

Within the singular measure of a heartbeat; without pause
    Within breath; vacant of hesitation
My desire, alight
For there is no other girl I love
For it's you, and only you.

For you are the missing piece from my heart
No further need I search
For the lost, now found.

PALPABLE

To see the sleep in your eyes, your hair, untamed
To hug you, to hold you close and tight.

Subtly

A kiss upon your forehead.

Softly

A kiss upon your lips.

Intimately

To hold your cheeks between thine hands
To lay but a butterfly kiss, upon your nose.

Passionately

Thy hands cupping and lifting
With devilish grin and twinkle in thy eye.

The intimacy… palpable
  The passion… absolute
    The romance… undeniable

PASSION. INTIMACY. LOVE

Just three words…
Two beating hearts…
One solemn promise…

A lifetime filled with memories, of ups and downs
Of laughter and tears.

Just you and me.

TOUCH

You touched my soul in a way it never had before
    You awoke my mind from its slumber
You reignited my passion from its smouldering embers
    You showed me, I could love forevermore

I long for the moment; your touch upon my body, in ways
    I've never been touched before

SERENDIPITOUS

A serendipitous moment… one woman, one man…
Two souls, meandering. Two hearts, searching.
A serendipitous blessing, perhaps.

Two paths intersecting
Unbeknownst, the years past
How close, yet so far
Destinations shared in imprint, timing, slightly adrift.

The green… the gold
The passion and the beauty -- two souls entwined
Two spirits dancing
Two hollow rings, one promise.

Uninhibited.
Passionate.
Unbridled.
Exotic.
Real.

PROMISES

I promise to never do you harm, to hold your hand in mine
To walk kerbside each time we're out and about, to absorb your smile
To gaze upon the Milky Way, nestled by the ocean shore
    To cuddle with you as you fall asleep
To wipe away your tears
To hug you tight, each time we must depart
To kiss you as the sun slowly rises and again, as it slowly sets
To passionately love, absent of restraint
To be with you, no matter what life may throw our way To protect you.

Together, there isn't anything we cannot do.

THREE MINUTES

"I'll always be there when you wake"

One hundred and eighty seconds...
Desiring eyes, intense in gaze
Synchronicity of two hearts
Two souls craving one connection
Two bodies hunger for just one touch
Just three minutes... a momentary gaze
Two heartbeats align... one rhythm

HEART'S DESIRE

She possesses the gentlest of souls
She carries a fantastical spirit
She owns the warmest of hearts.

She's been hurt… she's been pained, and yet, she remains unchanged; pure.

Her heart beats with enthusiastic rhythm, resonating her energy while radiating her warmth
For what she deserves, is that of her desires
Someone who'll cherish her
    Someone who'll adore her
Someone who'll protect her heart
    Someone who'll never try to change her
Someone who'll fight for her
    Someone who'll champion her
Someone who'll love her for the woman she is
    Someone who'll never leave
The one… who'll always choose her.

ONE

One second… four babies are born.

One minute… blood circulates our entire body, three times.

One hour… forty million people are enjoying sex.

One moment… life can change.

One day… the sun will disappear.

One day… no longer will you see these blue eyes.

One day… this voice will fall silent.
One day… these words will be lost.

One day… I'll be gone.

One life… one heart.

One moment… defining.

One is that of loneliness.

I WANT YOU

I want to be the one who brings a smile to your face
I want to be the one who brings a glint to your eye

I want to be the one on your mind when you awaken from
    your slumber
I want to be the one on your mind when you fall into your
    dreams

I want to feel your hand inside of mine
I want to gaze into your chocolaty eyes
I want to wrap my arms around you
I want to kiss your sweet lips

LONELY HEART

The sound of her laugh… the desire in her eyes.

The passion of her words… the intensity in her eyes.

The striking figure she cuts… the energy she radiates.

Her beautiful smile, alluring
Her compassion and empathy, contagious.
Her soul, warm.
Her heart, home.

To but feel her skin of silk
To but kiss her supple lips
To taste her sweet nectar
To but hold her close
To but feel her breath upon my face
To but hear the rhythm of her heart.

And yet…
A wistful heart, and an empty bed.

Printed in the USA
CPSIA information can be obtained
at www.ICGtesting.com
CBHW030411270824
13760CB00009B/416